Masters of Music
ILLUSTRATED BY RICHARD SHIRLEY SMITH
TCHAIKOVSKY

In the same series

HANDEL
MOZART
BEETHOVEN
DEBUSSY
BRITTEN

Masters of Music
TCHAIKOVSKY

Percy M. Young

Ernest Benn · London
David White · New York

FIRST PUBLISHED 1968
BY ERNEST BENN LIMITED
BOUVERIE HOUSE · FLEET STREET
LONDON · EC4
& DAVID WHITE
60 EAST 55TH STREET · NEW YORK · NY10022

© PERCY M. YOUNG 1968
ILLUSTRATIONS © ERNEST BENN LIMITED 1968

PRINTED IN GREAT BRITAIN

SBN 510-13734-2

LIBRARY OF CONGRESS CATALOG CARD NUMBER
68-9037

Contents

	PREFACE	7
1.	*Russia in the Nineteenth Century*	11
2.	*Middle-class Education*	17
3.	*Late Developer*	22
4.	*The Dedicated Composer*	29
5.	*A Patroness*	37
6.	*Fame in the Future?*	45
7.	*"The Hermit of Klin"*	53
8.	*The Conductor*	57
9.	*Master of Ballet*	65
	INDEX	75

Preface

IF A VOTE WERE TAKEN among the general body of music-lovers to determine the relative popularity of the greater musicians it is likely that Tchaikovsky would come at the top of the list. If the process could be extended back to the beginning of this century it is certain that he would win by a large margin. Among professional musicians and critics, however, the verdict would be less favourable. We may, therefore, conclude that Tchaikovsky possessed certain qualities and was deficient in others.

The strongest characteristic of Tchaikovsky's music is its capacity to reflect feelings, and it is evident in many ways; for instance, in the shaping of melodies, the choice of rhythms, the apparently spontaneous application of telling harmonies, the wide range of dynamics, and the nature and compulsion of the orchestral colouring. Adding these things together we arrive at the kind of music that we, if we were thinking of becoming composers, might feel like composing. It is, in a sense, within our compass of understanding because it seems to represent what we ourselves are. By the same token, it is music that lacks the more abstract qualities of, say, Bach or Beethoven.

A composer is the child of his time. Tchaikovsky was the first notable composer to be acknowledged as a world master during his lifetime—his fame extending from the Caucasus to the banks of the Hudson River. He was the first to feel the potential of a vast audience, of a great mass of music-lovers rather than of a narrowly aristocratic, or limited middle-class, minority. We can see the shape of things to come in the story of Tchaikovsky's public life, which became increasingly significant to more and more people. A sign of this was the repetition of one of his concerts, in 1887, by the Moscow Music Society, for which the price of tickets was reduced to admit those of limited means. Tchaikovsky was delighted at the way in which this audience, unaccustomed to such music, listened to his works.

Of the inner thoughts of composers who lived before the nineteenth century we know little more than is revealed in their music. And this despite the accumulation of documents that has gone on. The nineteenth century was a great age of letter-writing. Tchaikovsky himself was a compulsive correspondent (he also kept a copious diary) and there are thousands of his letters still in existence. Those in which he spoke most freely—on all kinds of subjects—were to members of his family. Of these letters, covering his life from his student days until shortly before his death, there are almost a thousand in existence. From them we learn of Tchaikovsky's likes and dislikes so far as people, nations, poets, novelists, and painters, were concerned. We also learn of the duality of his nature. Aware of this duality—which afflicted him in many ways—Tchaikovsky was unable to come to terms with it. In this his was a tragic life, though, as he himself often put it, "with delightful moments". At this point we begin to realise that this duality is expressed in his music, which, like his life, is—as the composer Shostakovich points out—truly tragic in the larger meaning of the word.

In this connection two phrases from Tchaikovsky's pen are worth noting. The first, written when he was busy with the opera *Eugene Onegin* in 1878, is: "To be sorry for the past, to hope for the future, never to be content with the present—that is my life." The second, from the same year, was the consequence of reading Schiller's play about Joan of Arc: "I suddenly felt so sorry for the whole of mankind."

Tchaikovsky was a Russian—considered by Tchekov to be only second in greatness to Tolstoi—and deeply patriotic. Sometimes he was ashamed of the contrasts of life in Russia, and of the stupidities and injustices of which the Czarist government was guilty. He spoke out on these matters, for he was a humane man. Like his sister Alexandra he had uncanny visionary powers, and it sometimes seems, both from his music and his letters, that he had some kind of premonition of the catastrophe that was to befall his country, and indeed members of his own family circle. Nonetheless he deemed it his duty to serve his country. This he did by composing music which is Russian (as will be explained), but which also belongs to the whole western world. More, perhaps, than any other man he built a bridge where one was, and is, needed. He loved his own people, but he never lost sight of "the whole of mankind".

I am grateful to have been able to talk about Tchaikovsky and his friends with Mme Galina von Meck, his niece, through whose kindness I have been able to see letters of the composer not as yet generally accessible.

P.M.Y.

1. *Russia in the Nineteenth Century*

SO FAR AS THE REST OF THE WORLD is concerned Peter Ilyich Tchaikovsky is the greatest, and most popular, of all Russian composers. In terms of music he is, as it is said, "the spirit of Russia". At the same time his music is highly personal. It is, we may feel, the man himself. But at the same time it suggests human feelings in general. One is aware that this music, filled with emotion, has a powerful effect on the emotions. Since certain works, such as the ballets, the Fourth, Fifth, and Sixth Symphonies, and the First Piano Concerto, enjoy an immense popularity, we tend to take them for granted. It should not be forgotten, however, that when they were new they were very new, startling by their modernity, daring in their innovations, and not always readily understood.

On the surface the works of Tchaikovsky with which we are familiar have points of contact with other familiar types of music. Tchaikovsky was a composer of symphonies (six in all), concertos (three for piano, and one for violin, and orchestra), and chamber music, which were derived from classical Austrian/German principles. He was a master of ballet, in which there is a strong French influence. As a composer of opera he was in debt to the great Italian tradition. European music in all its forms helped to shape Tchaikovsky's music. But its spirit, its power, its individuality, stemmed from the cultures of Moscow and St Petersburg (Leningrad), from the history of the many peoples who belonged to Russia, and, most of all, from Tchaikovsky's personality and the relationship between that personality and the world around him.

Until the eighteenth century Russia was an almost unknown country. It became a Great Power under the rule of Peter the Great, whose mission it was both to strengthen his country and to establish strong connections between it and the western countries. He extended trade; re-modelled his army on the Austrian pattern, and civil administration after the Prussian manner; and encouraged his ruling class, at least, to draw abreast of western culture by studying French philosophy, English literature and science, and Italian and German music. The processes of Peter the Great were carried several stages further by Catherine the Great, the ruler of Russia from 1762 to 1796. During this period St Petersburg, founded by Peter, became — as it still is — one of the show cities of Europe.

The rulers of Russia were absolute monarchs. Their word was law. So too was that of their representatives, in the army, in the Civil Service, in the judiciary. The leading positions in the State were occupied by members of the aristocracy. Those who were not of aristocratic birth but who reached positions of power became aristocratic by adoption. The well-to-do had fine houses in the cities, and large estates in the country. They became European rather than Russian, were often intolerant to their inferiors, and frequently and openly corrupt.

The great mass of Russian people lived away from the cities, and worked on the land. They lived, under feudal conditions and without any kind of freedom, as serfs. The contrasts as between the ruling class and the rest were more

marked in Russia, and such subject countries as Finland and Poland, than anywhere else in Europe. It needed very little to stir revolution.

As it happened the spirit of revolution was stimulated by events in France at the end of the eighteenth century. Those who were first moved to point to injustice and to act against it in Russia were not the peasants (on whom controls were severe) but progressive members of the educated élite. Just before Christmas in 1825 an insurrection broke out in the army. This was organised by a number of officers who had plotted in secret (because open discussion was impossible and illegal) to establish a national assembly. The insurrection was beaten down, and its leaders were executed, or banished to Siberia. One family prominent in the "Decembrist Revolution", the Davydovs, was to be related to that of the Tchaikovskys through marriage.

Those who were inspired by revolutionary ardour were nationalists. They wished Russian intellectual and artistic activity to draw on the native qualities of the Russian people, as told in many legends, and as shown in the realm of folk-art and folk-music. The time was ripe, then, for a period of creativity.

In the first half of the nineteenth century Russian literature, in all forms, was enriched by the works of Alexander Pushkin (1799–1837), Ivan Turgeniev (1818–83), Feodor Dostoevski (1821–81), and others; and music by the operas and ideals of Mikhail Glinka (1803–57) and Alexander Dargomizhsky (1813–69). Both Glinka and Dargomizhsky worked in close association with the writers of their time, and they introduced into their operas the idioms of folk-music. Neither composer pleased the majority of fashionable opera-goers of his day, for, as always, the rich people who dictated fashion disliked change. They were content with Italian opera. The new kind, furnished by Glinka and Dargomizhsky, being revolutionary in one way was thought likely to be revolutionary in another.

Nonetheless these composers exercised a profound influence, which affected the next generation of Russian musicians.

Glinka and Dargomizhsky were wealthy. For a time each held a post in the Civil Service, which, attracting young men who wished to mix in influential circles and yet have time on their hands to devote to other interests, was a regular breeding-ground for artists of one sort or another.

Another member of the Civil Service contemporary with those two composers was Ilya Petrovich Tchaikovsky, a mining engineer who ended his career as principal of an institute of technology.

In upper-class families the matter of ancestry is taken to be important. So long as a sense of antiquity can be suggested it does not greatly matter whether distant ancestors were conspicuous for their qualities or their defects. To the respectable Tchaikovskys it was something to be able to boast that far away in the misty past there was one of their name (or, almost of their name) who was a villain. The legendary founder of the family was a Cossack, from the Urals. His name was Tchaika (which means "gull"). He was, like all men of his tribe, a man of courage and determination, but without much respect for law. He was, so it was believed, once convicted of robbery with violence, and condemned to death. He was, however, reprieved; and then, intending to turn over a new leaf, he changed his name to Tchaikovsky.

Ilya Petrovich Tchaikovsky had none of the valour of his

remote ancestor. He was a sensitive man, with limited ambitions, and a talent for managing his affairs rather badly. He was, relatively speaking, frequently short of money. Tchaikovsky married a German woman, by whom he had a daughter. After her death he married Alexandra Assière, of French parentage. Of this marriage there were six children: Nicholas, Peter Ilyich, Alexandra (who bore her mother's name), Hippolyte, and the twin brothers, Anatoli and Modest. Until 1850 the Tchaikovskys lived in Kamsko-Vatinsk (province of Viatka). In that year they moved to St Petersburg. As was the custom in their class of society the Tchaikovsky children were much in the care of servants, and their education was attended to in the first place by governesses.

Peter stood out by reason of his high intelligence, his winsome manner, his musical aptitude, and his nervous temperament. His father lacked assurance. His mother suffered from time to time from what was described as epilepsy. Peter inherited his mother's tendency to nervous disorders, but he looked to her for a sense of security that he did not find in his father. When he was fourteen his mother died (his father married for a third time in 1865) and this had a profound effect on the course of his life.

2. Middle-class Education

AS HE GREW UP, TCHAIKOVSKY—without a mother—held tight to the bonds of affection that existed within his family. To some extent his sister Alexandra, although younger, took the place of his mother, while towards his younger brothers, particularly the twins, he acted almost maternally. This is shown in the hundreds of letters, still in existence, which he wrote to them. Because of his innate, and inherited, sensitivity, and because of the position in which he found himself in respect of his sister and brothers, he was never able to enjoy normal relationships with other people in adult life. He was also permanently haunted by a sense of inward fear, which became the more intense as he found his vocation in music.

Although musical there was no idea when he was a boy that he should become a musician. In the class of society to which he belonged a career in music was not to be thought of, and, since the notable composers of Russia already mentioned were amateurs and not professionals, there were no precedents to give encouragement. But the germ of music was working within him. He had had piano lessons since he was seven which led him towards the conventional classics; but at the back of his mind, forever playing on his imagination, were the folk-songs he had heard as a small child in the country.

For nine years Tchaikovsky was a pupil at the Law School in St Petersburg. He was interested enough in music to join the choral society there, and to continue with his piano

lessons. He even tried his hand at composition, but, feeling insecure in the basic techniques, did not pursue it. At the age of seventeen he left the Law School and satisfied his father at least by being appointed as a clerk to the legal department of the Civil Service. If not over-enthusiastic he was determined to take his duties seriously. Judging by the periods of absence he allowed himself and by the manner in which he threw himself into a gay life it would seem that he was stronger in resolution than in performance.

At the end of 1860 Alexandra married Leo Davydov, son of a Decembrist who had suffered banishment. She went to live on an estate in the province, and near the city, of Kiev, and in the next year a daughter was born. Tchaikovsky wrote frequently, and when he could he went to stay with his sister and brother-in-law, finding relaxation in their company and on their estate. He was devoted to, and loved by, his niece, and in due course by her brothers and sister. This affection for children, which was always returned, was one of the most endearing of Tchaikovsky's characteristics. In the course of time there were many children, not directly related to him, who called him "Uncle Peter".

The year 1861 was decisive. Tchaikovsky went to the theatre, he read many books, he talked long into the night with intellectual and artistic friends. He listened to operas — by Rossini, Verdi, Mozart, Auber, Meyerbeer, Donizetti and Bellini — and he studied singing by sitting in at the lessons of a famous teacher named Piccioli. Acting as a kind of secretary to an engineer friend of his father he was able to visit Germany, France, and England. With some knowledge of foreign languages — in which he was always interested, though it took a long time for him to make his English serviceable — he was expected to act as interpreter. This tour, at an impressionable age, on top of his existing interest in European culture, gave him a European outlook. Throughout his life he travelled much in western Europe. Even though he always said that he wanted to do nothing more than return to "Holy Russia", or "Mother Moscow", he was not among those who considered that a narrow nationalism was the answer to all problems. This made

him critical of artists and composers who believed that it was.

A patriot, Tchaikovsky believed in natural progress rather than in revolution. In the spring of 1861 the Czar granted a Declaration of Freedom for the serfs. Tchaikovsky went to church, "to see what impression it would make on the peasants," and to the Opera to hear the acclamations of the packed audience for the Czar. A liberal humanist, Tchaikovsky believed that the peasants should be free, and also that it was his duty to praise the generosity (as he took it) of the Czar. In such matters he was, no doubt, naïve; but he cared for justice in society and for kindness in the maintenance of justice.

Meanwhile, music was claiming more and more of his attention. He began to take regular lessons in theory, and in the autumn of 1862 he became a student at the newly founded School of Music in St Petersburg, of which the Director was Anton Rubinstein (1830–94). Rubinstein, world-famous as pianist and a successful composer in an acceptable German style, exercised a strong influence on Tchaikovsky, who soon realised that he had to make a choice. Music, he wrote to his sister in 1863, was all that he was good at. "I must give up everything else to develop and to cultivate the germ that God has planted in me." In respect of his Civil Service career he had more integrity than many of his colleagues. He pointed out that it was immoral to accept a salary for life without doing anything to merit it. With his father's blessing, but not with his entire approval, he resigned his post and dedicated himself to his vocation.

Dedication is the word. The times were not propitious. Tchaikovsky's father was on the point of retiring from his last appointment, and was deeply in debt. Peter had to live as best he could on limited means. He also had to make up for lost time by working hard. Indeed, he overworked, often sitting at his table through the night to finish the exercises set for him by Rubinstein. It is worth noting that among the tasks undertaken at this time was a translation of a recently published book on orchestration by the Belgian scholar François Gevaert (1828–1908).

3. Late Developer

AMONG THE GREAT COMPOSERS Tchaikovsky was a late starter. And when, at the age of twenty-one, he began to attempt more or less large-scale works he met with considerable discouragement. Rubinstein was a severe critic and when, at his suggestion, Tchaikovsky composed an overture based on *The Storm*, a play by Alexander Ostrovsky (1823–86), Rubinstein refused to accept it as a passable examination entry. Despite this rebuff Tchaikovsky persisted. In 1865 a set of dances for orchestra was given a performance in Pavlosk. These dances were later used for ballet in the opera *Voevoda*, a work which was also based on a play by Ostrovsky. In his last year at the School of Music Tchaikovsky composed a String Quartet in B flat (of which only a fragment remains), an Overture in F, for small orchestra, and—for his diploma work—a setting of Schiller's *Ode to Joy* (Beethoven set this poem in the "Choral" Symphony) for soloists, chorus, and orchestra. Tchaikovsky conducted the overture himself—unwillingly, for he was ill at ease on the concert platform. When the *Ode to Joy* was performed the composer, his health impaired by hard work and irregular and uncomfortable living conditions, was not present. The future, on the whole, did not look bright.

Meanwhile, in Moscow, Nicholas Rubinstein (1835–81) was looking for teachers for the School of Music there of which he was the Director. Having heard of Tchaikovsky and seen some of his work he invited him to join his staff—as a teacher of harmony—at a salary of 600 roubles (which

was doubled at the end of the first year; at that time 10 roubles equalled £1). For Tchaikovsky this was the break he had been looking for. It was not that the salary was spectacular, nor that the work was particularly interesting; but an official appointment was some justification for his having renounced the Civil Service. His father, however, now living in retirement far away in the Urals, took a poor view of the situation. Observing that Peter had a fine brain, and had enjoyed a first-class education, he described the salary offered as an insult. With some bitterness he went on to point out that the only people who did well out of music in Russia were popular Italian opera composers. Verdi, he said, could ask and receive 30,000 roubles for an opera.

Tchaikovsky was fortunate in that Nicholas Rubinstein —

who allowed him a rent-free room in his house—appreciated his talents. Since Rubinstein was the director of the fortnightly Musical Society Concerts—a feature of Moscow musical life—this meant that opportunities were likely to open up. Within two or three years Tchaikovsky was well-known to the musical connoisseurs of Moscow. His personal charm won him many friends, and he began to be able to report successes in the concert-room to his family. Often he thought he had had more success than he had. Among the works composed at this time were an Overture on the Danish National Anthem, a symphonic poem entitled "Fate", a symphony, and the opera *Voevoda*.

The "Danish" Overture (op. 15) was commissioned by Rubinstein for a State visit to Moscow of the Grand Duke Alexander and his Danish bride, Princess Dagmar. It is interesting as the first example of the pageant-type music designed to catch the patriotic ear at which Tchaikovsky became expert. "Fate"—the idea runs throughout the music of the nineteenth century—was more ambitious than credible, and was badly received by the critics. It was dedicated to Mily Balakirev (1837–1910), who, without much enthusiasm, conducted it in St Petersburg. The first Moscow performance was marked by an unfavourable notice by the critic Hermann Laroche (1845–1904), a former fellow student with and friend of Tchaikovsky. He complained that the work showed too much German influence. The same critic also took apart the opera *Voevoda* (op. 3), which had five performances at the Bolshoi Theatre, and was then withdrawn. As for the symphony, which was entitled "Winter Daydreams" (op. 13), this was unsuccessful in St Petersburg, but warmly applauded in Moscow. In this symphony —in which Russian folk-melodies were used—Tchaikovsky

showed for the first time the originality of his method of selecting and blending tone-colours.

During these years in Moscow the climate of musical criticism was changing, largely through the enthusiasm of the strong nationalist group led by Balakirev. Laroche's condemnation of Tchaikovsky's German tendencies was symptomatic. The same critic defined a new attitude when he wrote a series of articles in 1867-8 in which the importance of Glinka in Russian music was emphasised. Tchaikovsky had for some time been deeply interested in the music of Glinka and this is illustrated by an anecdote that also serves to show one side of his personality.

In the spring of 1866 there was an attempt on the life of the Czar. In the evening of the day on which the news reached Moscow Tchaikovsky went to the Bolshoi Theatre to see the opera *A Life for the Czar*. This opera tells of the Polish patriots who took up arms against the Russians in 1612. The assassination attempt of 1866 was plotted also by Poles. During the performance of the opera at the Bolshoi the appearance of the Polish soldiers on the stage caused uproar. The audience shouted "Down with the Poles". At the end of the performance a portrait of the Czar—Alexander II—was brought on the stage, and there were violent scenes of enthusiasm. The music was quite forgotten by all save one. Tchaikovsky, aloof from the hysteria of the crowd, sat in his seat with his head bowed over Glinka's score, which he had borrowed from the library of the Musical Society. His neighbours took a poor view of his apparent lack of patriotism.

A further incentive to progressive musicians and critics to move away from the influences of German musical style was provided by the occasion of the visit to Moscow in 1867 of Hector Berlioz (1803-69). At an official dinner given in his honour Tchaikovsky was called upon to make a speech. This, in which he paid high tribute to the visiting composer, was delivered in French.

Tchaikovsky enjoyed Moscow in so far as it enabled him to make the acquaintance of interesting and influential people, and for the opportunities afforded him of earning a living and hearing his music performed, but he often longed for St Petersburg, or the wooded countryside of Kamenka where his sister lived. Being still hard up for funds he found his life restricted in some ways. An avid reader of English books—at this time he was especially addicted to Charles Dickens's *Pickwick Papers*, of which, in one letter, he wrote a perceptive criticism—he would have liked to join the English Club. But he could not afford the subscription. In general he deplored the dullness and the conservative habits of thought of Moscow society.

In 1868 he found a congenial companion in the Belgian singer Désirée Artôt. Tchaikovsky, shy but charming, gentle in manner but lively in conversation, was a natural target for young women. He had his admirers among his girl students. Désirée Artôt fell for his charms and having pursued him brought him to believe that he was in love. They talked of marriage (and Tchaikovsky wrote of its probability in letters to his family); but Artôt insisted on her own terms. Nothing must interfere with her career as a *prima donna*. Tchaikovsky, alarmed by the thought that he would, as he said, become "the husband of his wife", took avoiding action. In the meantime the lady, having gone to sing in Warsaw, met and married a Spanish singer of a suitably accommodating disposition. Tchaikovsky, whose involvement had caused concern to his friends, was congratulated on his deliverance from what everyone feared would be an unhappy match. Nevertheless Tchaikovsky continued to have a strong affection for the singer and he never failed to praise her great gifts. A set of six songs (op. 63) were dedicated to her.

At this time Tchaikovsky was working on another opera—*Undine*. This romantic story, by the German writer Friedrich Fouqué (1773–1843), had also served as the basis of operas by Ernst Hoffmann (1776–1822) and Albert Lortzing (1801–51). Having finished his score in the summer of 1869 Tchaikovsky sent it to St Petersburg—where it was rejected by the directors of the Imperial Opera. In 1870 a selection of numbers from the first Act were given in Moscow in concert form. But the composer, always economical of his ideas, used up some of the material in later works. A love duet became Odette's *Adagio* in the second Act of *Swan Lake*; a bridal procession was turned into the slow movement of the Second Symphony. Having saved what he considered to be the best of yet another ill-fated opera Tchaikovsky destroyed the rest.

We may now see the direction in which Tchaikovsky's music was moving: towards ballet and opera, symphonic poem, and symphony. The narrative influences that lay behind music for the theatre also affected that for the concert-room. Tchaikovsky—a true Romantic in this—intended that his music should express his views on life in general, and on his own in particular. He also believed that music should follow certain accepted principles, and that it should, as he said, be "beautiful". This often brought him into conflict with the nationalists—whose works he frequently considered badly composed. In one of his letters of 1877 he wrote: "Up to now we tried to charm people by music, now one tortures and exhausts them." It may be that this can be read as relevant to our own times.

4. *The Dedicated Composer*

TCHAIKOVSKY'S MUSICAL ATTITUDES are explained by his likes and dislikes, not only in respect of music—so far as music was concerned he was a firm believer in the importance of perfection of form. He strove unceasingly to this end and when his Second Symphony, in C minor (op. 17), approved by Laroche, was successfully launched in 1872, he remarked that its form was more nearly perfect than that of any other of his existing works. On the other hand this work was contrary to the idea that symphony is "absolute" music (that is, entirely independent and self-sufficient), for it incorporated folk-songs from the Ukraine.

About the tune that is the basis of the finale there is an entertaining, and enlightening anecdote. The composer was staying with the Davydovs when he was working on the last movement. As was his habit, he composed at the piano; he played over what he had written, or what he was going to write. One day he played the melody of "The Crane", the germ of the melody of which is shown in Ex. 1—the exciting introduction to the finale. The butler came in and said, "Excuse me, sir, you have got the tune wrong—it goes like this." He sang it and the way in which he sang it is reflected, so it was said, in the course of the movement which is, in effect, a series of 18 variations on "The Crane". The form in which the Second Symphony (popularly known as "the little Russian") is now heard is the revised version of 1879.

Ex. 1

The idea of a folk-song symphony related to two other principles held by Tchaikovsky. One was that music should be lyrical, i.e. based on song: the other that it should be informative. This example shows Tchaikovsky's love of a theatrical gesture—in the explosive *fortissimo*, the rests, the pauses, the switches of tonality, and the placing of the drum-roll.

He found his greatest pleasure in the theatre and in literature. He loved opera (although he was very critical of standards of performance and production), asking only that the subject should be clear and simple (if it was lyrical so much the better), the vocal parts eminently singable and the orchestration vivid, evocative, and effectively descriptive. In the period in which he was coming to maturity he wrote appreciatively of Verdi's *Aida*, Weber's *Der Freischütz*, Cherubini's *The Water-Carrier*, and Bizet's *Carmen*. When he heard Wagner's *Ring* in 1876 he complained that as a whole it was boring, that the vocal parts were colourless, that the harmonies were "muddled". The *Rhinegold* he described as an "impossible medley" but one through which there shimmered "extremely beautiful details". On the

The Dedicated Composer

whole, though, if this was, as people said, the music of the future he was not much in favour of it. We may now wonder at Tchaikovsky's apparent lack of perception. If we do we should bear in mind that at the present time—also one of great change—there are just as many people who might be expected to know better making equally doubtful judgements. If opera intrigued Tchaikovsky so also did ballet. In this field the work he loved above all others was *Sylvia* by Léo Delibes (1836–91), which he said he liked a hundred times more than Wagner's *Ring*.

During this part of his life Tchaikovsky was overworked, and he was perpetually hard up. He taught at the Conservatorium without much enthusiasm. From 1876 he wrote articles for the *Moscow News*—characteristically farming out some of them to his brother Modest, whom he encouraged towards a literary career in the belief that he had great talent in this direction. He was also generous in helping Modest financially. The one luxury he allowed himself was a valet (which makes strange reading today), whose name was Alesha, and with whom he was on very close terms of friendship. Although regarding himself as a good citizen of Moscow (he began to speak of St Petersburg with distaste) Tchaikovsky was rarely in one place. He moved his rooms in the city, he went to stay with his sister whenever he could; he took every chance of visiting western Europe. It was so all his life. He was, as one of his relatives lately remarked, a "wanderer". But he composed incessantly.

The Second Symphony was followed by that sometimes known as the "Polish". (Poland was at that time regarded—also by Tchaikovsky—as a part of Russia.) The Third Symphony (op. 29), first performed at the beginning of 1876, was well received, not only in Moscow, but also all over

Europe. The principal key of this symphony is that of D minor, in which the introduction of the first movement establishes a tragic mood in *tempo di marcia junebre*. Here, again, is the idea of "Fate". The Polish character of the struggle against "Fate" is acknowledged at the beginning of the finale in the words *tempo di polacca*. In view of the fact that this symphony is rarely played today it is interesting to notice that César Cui (1835—1918), one of the nationalist composers and also a critic, wrote that while this was a good work it should only be regarded as a prelude to greater works to come. "We have," he wrote in the St Petersburg newspaper, "a right to expect more of Mr Tchaikovsky." Within the field of classical forms Tchaikovsky composed two more String Quartets (op. 22 and op. 30) and the First Piano Concerto in B flat minor (op. 23).

It is safe to say that this is the most popular piano concerto ever written. Some critics have supposed that because of this it also must be the worst. There is no need to agree with such critics—but before giving them the brush-off it is worth remembering that when Nicholas Rubinstein, Tchaikovsky's friend, heard the concerto for the first time he was extremely outspoken. So much so that Tchaikovsky took a long time to recover from what he considered to be an insult. Rubinstein, according to Tchaikovsky, poured out a torrent of words: the concerto was impossible to play, because of its many awkward passages; it was "ordinary and poorly composed", it was vulgar; sections had been lifted from the works of other composers—and so on. In the end Rubinstein recanted and played the concerto many times; but it was finally dedicated to Hans von Bülow (1830–94), the German pianist, who enjoyed great success with the work in the U.S.A., first performing it in Boston in 1875. At the same time the third String Quartet was also proving popular in the U.S.A.

The First Piano Concerto is away from the classical tradition of such works in that it displays a genius for theatrical presentation much more than for consistent musical argument, or development. It is a pageant of wonderful melodies, of effects of colour, of moods, of conflicts between the solo instrument and the orchestra. The way the music is laid out for the keyboard owes much to Franz Liszt (1811–86), for whose works Tchaikovsky had a high regard. So too does the manner in which themes are re-shaped, or (to use the conventional technical term) "metamorphosed".

It is not difficult to feel the spirit of folk-music behind this concerto. In fact, the main theme of the first movement is said to have been noted down by the composer from the singing of Ukrainian peasants at a country-fair (Tchaikovsky loved these fairs, and the side-shows which were a part of them) at Kamenka. The finale also begins with a Ukrainian dance theme.

During the nineteenth century the overture (properly belonging to the theatre) was developed for the concert-hall. The so-called "concert overture" was derived from the first-movement pattern of symphony, but made a vehicle of descriptive intention. The same tendency also led to the symphonic poem, and to the usually more loosely constructed fantasia. All these types belonged to the category of "programme music", and indicated music that was "about" something. When we use the word "about" in this connection we relate music to the functions of literature or the visual arts. It is easy to see why Tchaikovsky, a lover of the theatre, an avid reader, a keen connoisseur of art galleries and museums, and a student of folk-lore, was likely to be drawn more and more into this sphere of composition.

In 1869 Tchaikovsky composed his overture *Romeo and Juliet*, of which the subject was suggested to him by Balakirev. Three years later another Shakespearian theme—*The Tempest*—was similarly treated in an overture. In 1876 the fantasia *Francesca da Rimini* was produced. The last work was a by-product of opera (showing how close to the theatre such forms of music were), for Tchaikovsky was looking for an opera libretto. He was offered one by a poet named Zvanzev on the subject of Francesca (from Dante's *Inferno* V).

The Dedicated Composer

In composing this work Tchaikovsky acknowledged that in respect of the "storm" music he was greatly influenced by one of Gustav Doré's illustrations for the *Inferno*. In *Francesca* Tchaikovsky uses a very large orchestra, including three flutes, cor anglais, bass clarinet, tuba, side-drum, celesta, and harp, in addition to the normal "symphony orchestra" resources of the period. In this work we realise how truthfully Tchaikovsky spoke when he said that musical ideas came to him already existing in orchestral tone-colours.

Side by side with those works (not to mention some songs and piano pieces) Tchaikovsky was working at operatic projects—which met with little success. The directors of the Imperial Opera, in St Petersburg, were not very helpful to Russian opera, either refusing works, like Mussorgsky's *Boris Godunov*, because of their possible political implications (the censorship was very active), or, as in the case of Tchaikovsky, merely being generally obstructive. Tchaikovsky composed incidental music for Ostrovsky's *Snow Maiden* (op. 12, 1873)—a work which gave him great delight, and the operas, *The Oprichnik* (performed 1874) and *Vakula the Smith* (op. 14, performed 1876). In all of these works there was a strong flavour of national music; but none of them were of such commanding and universal appeal as that which he commenced in 1877—*Eugene Onegin* (op. 24), based on a poem by Pushkin. This was undertaken at the time when the composer had scored a a great success with the first of his ballets—*Swan Lake* (op. 20), planned originally as an entertainment for his nephews and nieces at Kamenka, and first performed at the Bolshoi Theatre, Moscow, on February 20, 1877. (The Russians still used the old-style Calendar, long given up in western Europe—where February 20 was March 4!)

Another work of this period which aroused great enthusiasm was Tchaikovsky's *Slavic March* (op. 31), a patriotic piece, based on Serbian tunes and ending with the Czar's Hymn, thus anticipating the *1812 Overture*. This piece was occasioned by the Serbo-Turkish War of 1876, and is worth hearing for the manner in which it conveys the wide range of the composer's emotions and of his means of expressing them.

5. *A Patroness*

A COMPOSER AS SENSITIVE AS TCHAIKOVSKY was deeply depressed by adverse criticism, and excessively elated by praise. As in music such as that of the *Slavic March*, so in his life he swung from one extreme to another. At one moment in his letters he could be gay, flippant, and light-hearted; at another unbearably, selfishly, gloomy and inward-looking. The adverse remarks of the Rubinsteins and Laroche (whom he knew well, and therefore took their strictures badly) sent him into a withdrawn state of melancholy. On the other hand the frequent kindness of Balakirev, Cui, Rimsky-Korsakov, and Mussorgsky (whose music he did not particularly like but thought the best of the nationalist school) surprised and elated him. His highest point of satisfaction, however, came in 1876 when he met the greatest, perhaps, of all Russian writers—Count Leo Tolstoi (1828—1910), and when Tolstoi paid him many compliments. The greatest of these was involuntary. During the performance of the first String Quartet (op. 11) Tchaikovsky and Tolstoi were sitting together. During the slow movement—a famous movement, known also in a version for string orchestra—Tolstoi burst into tears. The composer noted this in his diary with satisfaction. Tchaikovsky was prepared to overlook—what was common knowledge—that Tolstoi was quite unmusical.

At the end of 1876 Tchaikovsky received a letter from a Mme Nadezhda von Meck, the widow of a prosperous railway magnate, descended from an ancient family which had settled in Riga with the Teutonic Knights of the Middle

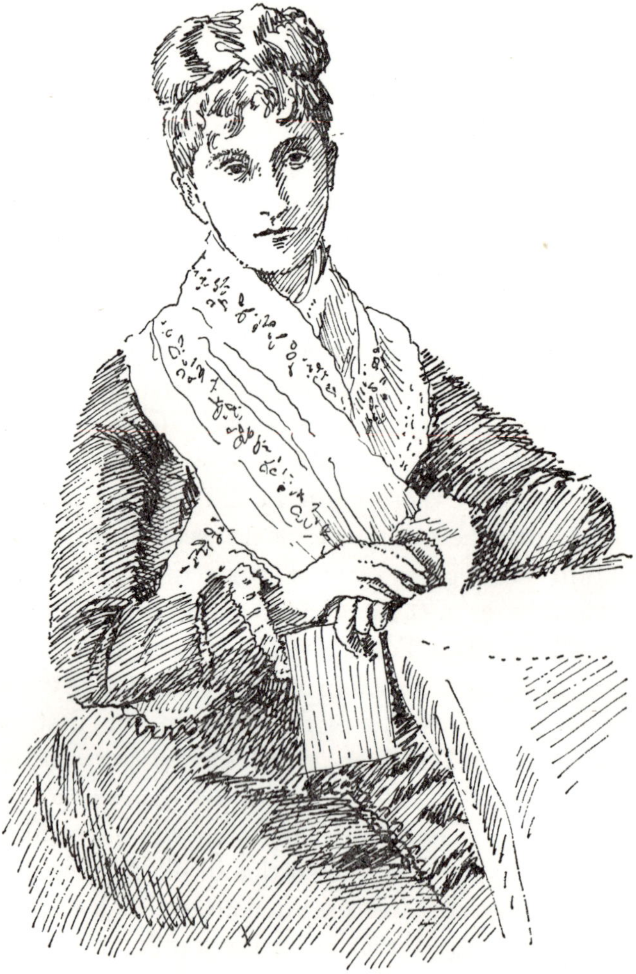

Ages. Mme von Meck inherited an enormous fortune after the death of her husband. She owned a fine mansion (with a special wing for guests) at Brailov in the Ukraine, and had a passion for music. Acquainted with the music of Tchaikovsky she wrote to him asking that he should arrange some pieces for violin and piano. This letter was the first in a series both to and from Tchaikovsky that has no parallel. The relationship between Mme von Meck and Tchaikovsky (she was nine years older) grew more and more intimate; but it existed only on paper—in the voluminous letters that have since been published.

In the early part of 1877 a pupil of Tchaikovsky, Antonina Milyukova, like others of his pupils, fell in love with him. She pursued him quite relentlessly, so that he gave way before her importunity and married her in July. This was a complete disaster. For reasons which have been stated Tchaikovsky found it difficult to establish normal relationships and the chance of his successfully undertaking marriage depended on a degree of understanding which Antonina did not possess. After three months, some part of which Tchaikovsky spent in Kamenka away from his wife, the ill-starred marriage broke up. Tchaikovsky, literally, ran away—from Moscow to St Petersburg. As the marriage collapsed so did Tchaikovsky, and his family were deeply concerned about his state of mind. He was, indeed, in the throes of a nervous breakdown.

Tchaikovsky was, of course, a conspicuous figure in Moscow. His ill-starred marriage was the talk of the city. Fortunately, there were those who had compassion for him, and Nicholas Rubinstein arranged that a special salary should be made available to him for his services to music in the Conservatorium and the city. This was to enable him to have long leave of absence. The doctors had prescribed a holiday in the West, and Anatoli Tchaikovsky had arranged to accompany his brother.

As usual there was the problem of money. What he received from the Conservatorium was something—but nothing like enough to support several expensive months in Italy and Switzerland, where, in any case, the rate of exchange was unfavourable to the rouble. Mme von Meck, having learned the whole story from Tchaikovsky—as well as others—offered to send him funds for his enforced vacation. Then she had a better idea: she would make him an annual allowance, so that he should be entirely free of financial worry. The arrangement, which contained the stipulation that the composer and his patroness should never meet, lasted for thirteen years, at the end of which Mme von Meck brought her bounty to an end rather more than abruptly.

During the period of his greatest depression Tchaikovsky was occupied on many projects. Before his marriage he had been working with delight on the greatest of his operas, *Eugene Onegin*, and also on the Fourth Symphony in F minor (op. 36), to become one of his most famous works. When he was abroad, first in Italy, and then in Switzerland, he gradually picked up the threads again. He had, indeed, a compulsion to compose, and the act of composing was in itself a kind of fulfilment of what life otherwise denied him. His music, so far as he was concerned, was his true self. The symphony was dedicated to Mme von Meck, and it was given its first performance in Moscow at the beginning of February, 1878. The conductor was Nicholas Rubinstein.

The composer was not present, but was beside himself with anxiety to discover how it had been received. It had been received with relative indifference. Mme von Meck, however, sent a telegram of warm congratulation. She followed this up with a letter in which she invited the composer to describe its significance. Is it, or is it not, she asked, programme music? Tchaikovsky wrote back at length, and his detailed account of the work makes an interesting comparison with the programme which Berlioz gave for his *Fantastic Symphony*. Both composers, the one near the beginning, the other near the end, of the nineteenth century, were concerned with the capacity of music to express the meaning, or the lack of meaning, of life. Whether music can do this is an open question. In the Romantic period there were many who believed that it could. Berlioz, Schumann, and Tchaikovsky gave some credibility to the belief.

The "metamorphosis" of themes has already been mentioned in connection with the First Piano Concerto. The Fourth Symphony begins with a striking theme, which recurs throughout the work. (Ex. 2.) This, wrote Tchai-

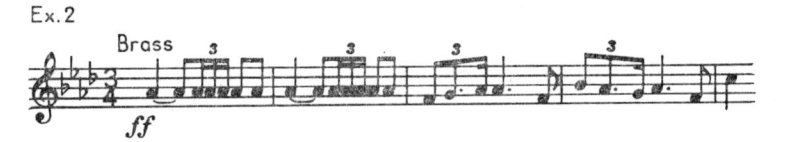

Ex. 2

kovsky, "is the germ of the whole symphony, without question its central idea. This is Fate, the fatal force that prevents our striving for happiness from succeeding. . . . It is invincible, it can never be mastered. One must submit to it and take refuge in futile longings." As has been seen "Fate" had already made one appearance in a major work of Tchaikovsky, but unaccompanied by the imaginative genius that is displayed in the symphony.

Why did the Fourth Symphony not meet with success at

once? Because many were obsessed (some still are) by the notion of an ideal symphony, a symphony in which proportion and musical logic should prevail over the expression of moods and feelings. Tchaikovsky also believed in the importance of well-made musical structures; but not at the expense of expression.

This symphony is theatrical in its gestures, in the character of its melodies, in the wealth of effects in the instrumentation, and, in the *pizzicato* effects of the third movement especially, it crosses the borders of ballet. This was pointed out to Tchaikovsky by Sergei Taneiev (1856–1915), whose opinion he generally valued. The element of dance—one of the two starting-points of music, the other being song—is very pronounced in Tchaikovsky's works. It is also the cause of many fascinating rhythmic insertions—as the change from $\frac{3}{8}$ to $\frac{2}{8}$ in the scherzo of the Second Symphony, the $\frac{5}{4}$ movements of *Sleeping Beauty* and the Sixth Symphony, and the many fascinating variations of the rhythmic structure of the waltz (see, for instance, Ex. 3). Tchaikovsky put up a spirited defence of ballet music, without conceding that his symphony was, in fact, "ballet", and protested against the implication that ballet music was music of an inferior nature. As for the introduction of dance motivs into symphonic music he appealed to Beethoven, "who frequently had recourse to such effects".

When he was in Clarens he spent some time with his former pupil, and Mme von Meck's "house musician", Yosif Kotek, a fine violinist. The presence of Kotek—whose devotion to Tchaikovsky was the first cause of Mme von Meck's interest in the composer—inspired Tchaikovsky to write for the violin. He composed a long but indifferent Sonata for violin and piano, and completed a vivacious

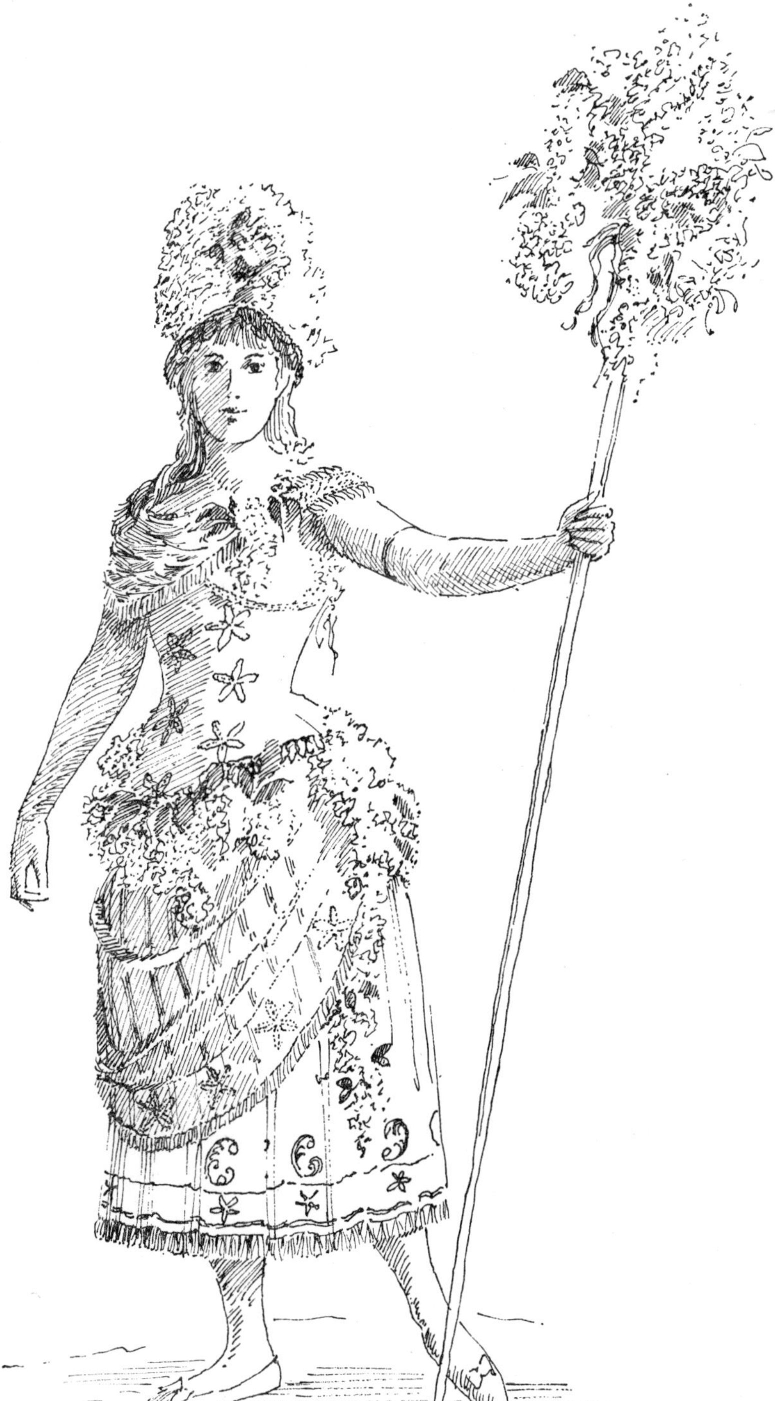

Valse-Scherzo (op. 34) for violin and small orchestra. This work, dedicated to Kotek, is a splendid example of Tchaikovsky's manipulation of instrumental colours, nothing being more effective than the happy placing of the notes of the single horn contained in the score. The work is light, gay, and infectious, and shows how strongly the composer was attracted to the waltz form.

Ex. 3

At the same time a far more important work was on the way. This was the Violin Concerto in D major (op. 35), which Kotek watched grow during the month of March 1878. When the movements were ready Kotek played them —with Tchaikovsky supplying the orchestral part on the piano. He played so well, said Tchaikovsky, that his first rendering was ready for the concert-room. The first and last movements were greeted with great enthusiasm by Kotek, the second *andante* movement with less. Tchaikovsky therefore removed this movement (which forms the third of the three violin pieces of op. 42 dedicated to Mme von Meck's estate at Brailov) and wrote another.

At this point it was time for him to return to Russia. He wanted to go, because, as usual when long absent, he was homesick. But he was nervous to return. And certainly he did not wish to go anywhere near Moscow. He went for a time to his sister's home and then gratefully accepted Mme von Meck's invitation to stay at Brailov—while she was away.

6. Fame in the Future?

WHILE HE WAS STAYING AT BRAILOV Tchaikovsky composed his *Children's Album* (op. 39), a set of 24 "easy pieces"—which are not quite as easy to play as they are to listen to. For delicacy and gentle humour these pieces, sometimes borrowing melodic as well as other ideas from Russia, Poland, France, Italy, and Germany, deserve a high place in the repertoire of the young pianist. They go excellently alongside the children's pieces of Robert Schumann, with which they have resemblances. These pieces were written for Tchaikovsky's favourite nephew, Vladimir (or "Bobyk"), to whom they were dedicated—although, as the composer wrote to his brother, the boy was not old enough to know what "dedicated" meant! The sensitivity of Tchaikovsky, which may sometimes be described as sentimentality, is beautifully shown in the hesitant movement, minor tonality, and downward movement of the broken melody of "The Poorly Doll". (Ex. 4.) In the next piece of the set the doll is buried to the strains of a miniature Funeral March, behind the plain, resonant, common chords of which may be sensed the music of the Russian Church. Tchaikovsky was always impressed by the ritual of the Church of which he was a member, and took immense pains when Alexander III asked him to compose liturgical works. The liveliest piece, perhaps, is the strident peasant's dance, which is (according to the title) to the accompaniment of the concertina (see Ex. 5). The chord marked *, which is a familiar discord, plays an important part in this piece. It gives a rough, vulgar,

Ex. 4

[musical notation: Moderato, Piano]

Ex. 5

[musical notation: mf]

character, entirely proper in this context. The piece indeed ends with this chord repeated seven times.

Some years later Tchaikovsky wrote a set of sixteen songs for children. While he was writing his piano pieces he also composed a work for his brother Anatoli—the six songs (four of them to poems by Tolstoi) of op. 38.

Music of this kind was an extension of his correspondence. Tchaikovsky found it difficult to express all he felt in words—and music often seems to have taken over where words left off. It should be remembered that a composer (a proper composer) is one to whom music is the first and most natural means of expression. In no case is this more true than in the case of Tchaikovsky.

After a restful period at Brailov Tchaikovsky went again to Switzerland—to Clarens, a little town on the lake of Geneva, which he liked very much. There he worked hard at the libretto and music of his opera *The Maid of Orleans*.

He read Schiller's play on the subject of Joan of Arc and other books as well. The story completely absorbed him and when he came back to Moscow early in 1879 for the first performance of *Eugene Onegin* he was able to bring with him the complete, but as yet unorchestrated, score of the new opera.

Eugene Onegin, performed by students of the Moscow Conservatorium, was not at first a great success. By now Tchaikovsky was beginning seriously to doubt whether he would ever make a real success. Certainly his music was widely played; but many critical voices were heard. When he went to hear a performance of *The Tempest* in Paris in 1879 he expected a cool reception. When it came — together with a few hisses of disapproval — he was not unprepared. He was even philosophical, writing to his brother Modest: "I know very well that my time will come in the future, but so much in the future that I will not see it in my lifetime."

He had reckoned without the First Piano Concerto. Even though critics in Vienna, Paris, and Berlin remained on the whole hostile this work was enjoying great success, especially in the United States. Hans von Bülow had introduced the work to the Americans, and it is interesting now to read a letter of his, written in 1875, in which he explained why he did so with conviction. Regarding Russia and the United States he said, "to my mind [these are] the only two parts of the world that are not played out." Tchaikovsky's music seemed to make a bridge between the two nations, and it was strengthened by the work of two conductors who were ardent supporters of the cause of Tchaikovsky. These were Karl Bergmann (1821–76) and Leopold Damrosch (1832–85), conductors respectively of the New York Philharmonic and New York Symphony Societies. The B flat minor Concerto was also rapturously received in London when it was played by Edward Dannreuther at one of the Crystal Palace concerts in 1876. By 1880 the work was established in the European repertoire.

In its own way the music of Tchaikovsky represented certain ideals of freedom. These were implicit in the folk-melodies which were at the roots of his inspiration, and in the character of his orchestration. The emotional quality of his works suggested the ideal — approved by Tchaikovsky when he read the works of Jean Jacques Rousseau (1712–1778) — of the right of the individual to be free. It was the lurking idea that the composer might be on the side of those who wished to change the existing order that caused demonstrations against his music, not infrequently in his own country.

Russia was a country under tyrannical rule. Those of liberal views suffered a continual sense of frustration and, when abroad, indignity. When he was in western Europe Tchaikovsky often noted the slights offered to Russian citizens. Once he remarked on the difference between France and Russia: the French way of life, he said, was more civilised. In 1879 an attempt was made on the life of Czar Alexander II (he was assassinated in 1881). In deep distress Tchaikovsky wrote to Mme von Meck: "So long as all of us — the citizens of Russia — are not called upon to take part in our country's government, there is no hope for a better future."

After the unsuccessful attempt on the life of the Czar the censorship, already strict, was tightened. Every opera libretto was gone through with a fine-toothed comb. A proposal to revive Tchaikovsky's *The Oprichnik* was vetoed on the grounds that it contained passages that could lead to sedition.

Fame in the Future?

Soon after this Nicholas Rubinstein died. For some time Tchaikovsky had been disturbed by attempts to destroy Rubinstein's authority in Moscow. This was a period in which there was a strong anti-Semitic feeling among the reactionary forces of Russia which led to a pogrom of Jews in 1881. That the Rubinsteins were Jewish was not in their favour. Tchaikovsky was entirely free of racial prejudice and while he had often disagreed with Nicholas Rubinstein he realised how much he owed to his encouragement. He was, therefore, greatly moved by Rubinstein's death, and the suggestion that he should take his place as Director of the Conservatorium caused him much heart-searching. He would have liked to have undertaken the work—but the claims of composition were not compatible with those of a demanding public office. So he eventually supported the claims of his former pupil Sergei Taneiev who had made a number of piano arrangements of his works.

During this period Tchaikovsky, worried by a chronic lack of money (despite Mme von Meck's generosity) and by the illness of his sister, was relatively inactive as a composer. But the works that he had accumulated were coming to life in concert-room and opera-house. *Eugene Onegin* proved more or less successful when performed at the Bolshoi Theatre, where, after the censor's ban was lifted, *The Oprichnik* was revived and enthusiastically welcomed, and *The Maid of Orleans* was given its première at the Marinsky Theatre in St Petersburg on February 25, 1881. The part of Dunois in this opera was taken by Fyodor Stravinsky, father of Igor Stravinsky. A young French musician, Claude Debussy (1863–1918), also a protégé of Mme von Meck, had made a piano duet version of some of the dances in *Swan Lake*. The songs and piano pieces of Tchaikovsky were taken up all over Russia by amateur musicians. The *Italian Capriccio* (op. 45), avowedly popular, took Moscow by storm, as also did the *Serenade for String Orchestra* (op. 48), at the beginning of 1882.

Two major works of this period received a mixed reception. The one was the Violin Concerto (op. 35) on which the composer had worked so hard with Kotek; the other the Second Pianoforte Concerto in G major (op. 44). Both were regarded as far too difficult, and the former especially too "barbarous". The Violin Concerto was intended to be played by the virtuoso player Leopold Auer (1845–1930). Auer (who settled in the U.S.A. after the 1917 Revolution in Russia) took one look at it and refused to play it. The first performance was given in New York in 1875 by Adolf Brodsky (1851–1929), who later migrated to Manchester, England, where he became leader of the Hallé Orchestra. Brodsky also introduced the Violin Concerto to Vienna and London, where it was received with tremendous enthusiasm. The conductor on both occasions was Hans Richter (1843–1916). Tchaikovsky was greatly cheered by these successes — and he returned to his reading of Dickens. At this time he was deep in *Bleak House*.

In the summer of 1882 an International Exhibition was held in Moscow, partly to draw attention to the quickening pace of Russian industrialization, and partly to inaugurate the reign of the new Czar, Alexander III. As part of this Exhibition a concert of Tchaikovsky's works, including the first performance of the new Piano Concerto (played by Taneiev), was given. Although the critics differed about the piano concerto the public gave the composer a hero's welcome. He was indeed the national composer of Russia, and nothing marked his status more than the *1812 Overture* (op. 49) which was played at this festival concert. Honoured by the Czar, Tchaikovsky was commissioned to compose a March for the Coronation, which duly appeared in time for the ceremony in 1883, and a Cantata entitled *Moscow*.

Expecting a substantial sum of money for the execution of the royal commission, Tchaikovsky was disgruntled when his only reward proved to be a large diamond ring. He pawned the ring, and then lost both the pawn ticket and the 375 roubles he had raised on his deposit.

This year was also notable for the fulfilment of an intention both of Tchaikovsky and Mme von Meck. They had, without consulting either of the persons concerned, decided that Mme von Meck's son, Nikolai Karlovich, should marry one of his nieces at Kamenka. They had selected Vera Davydov, but she thwarted their plans by following her own inclinations and marrying into the Rimsky-Korsakov family. Her place in respect of the von Meck alliance was taken by her sister Anna Lvovna, who was duly married to Nikolai Karlovich von Meck at the beginning of 1884.

7. "*The Hermit of Klin*"

AS HAS BEEN SEEN ALREADY Tchaikovsky (like most composers of that eminence) worked on several compositions at the same time, while at the back of his mind there always lay ideas for the future. A composer hopes for success maybe, but is rarely taken in by it. Nearly always it is the next work that is to be the one great achievement. This is part of the explanation of the restlessness of the composer's temperament. The same restlessness also distinguishes creative artists in other fields. In 1883 Tchaikovsky was reading a story by E. T. A. Hoffmann—*The Nutcracker and the Mouse King*. This story gave him much pleasure. It also gave him ideas, but these were not to take shape until some ten years later. Also that year Balakirev approached him, suggesting that he should write a symphonic work on the theme of Byron's *Manfred*, which had previously drawn a work from Schumann. Tchaikovsky's *Manfred* Symphony (op. 58) was composed in 1885 and performed in Moscow in the following year. But Tchaikovsky's main concern in 1883 and 1884 was for his new operatic project, *Mazeppa*, based on Pushkin's tragic tale *Poltava*. When this Ukrainian story of the seventeenth century was played both in Moscow and St Petersburg in 1884, its reception was lukewarm. The only crumb of comfort for the composer was the fact that the Czar had remained to the end of the St Petersburg performance. During that year Tchaikovsky was awarded the Order of St Vladimir by the Czar, who also honoured the composer by calling him to the Royal Box during a performance of *Eugene Onegin*. St Petersburg had taken this opera to its heart, and apart from Glinka's *A Life for the Czar*, no other Russian opera had achieved comparable popularity.

The core of *Eugene Onegin* is the famous scene in the first Act in which the heroine, Tatiana, writes a letter to Onegin. In this "letter-scene" Tchaikovsky shows not only his great lyrical gifts but also his perception of the state of mind of a young, impassioned, girl. A single phrase, in which the vocal part lies near the "whole-tone" scale, merging into an orchestral response, illustrates this.

Ex. 6

[Musical notation: Voice and Orch. parts, with text "Like an an-gel are you come?" and tone intervals marked above.]

A wanderer since his youth (the idea of "wandering" lies in the previous example), Tchaikovsky now particularly felt the need for a home of his own. More and more he longed for solitude—a theme that comes up time after time in his letters. In the spring of 1885 he found a home, once the property of a noble family but now in a state of decay, at Klin, near Maidanovo—convenient to Moscow and St Petersburg. He rented this house for a year; after that, loving the quiet countryside, he made it his permanent home.

In Klin Tchaikovsky lived a quiet life and followed a regular routine. After breakfast he read, corrected proofs, or composed until lunch-time. In the afternoons he went for long walks, as he did wherever he was living, whether at home or abroad. During his walks he thought about his work and often came back immediately to set down his thoughts on paper. These he kept and reconsidered the next day, making fuller sketches from his first notes. In the evenings he read, played the piano, or played cards. Although his habits led people to call him "the hermit of Klin" he was deeply concerned for the people who lived in the neighbouring village of Maidanovo.

Discovering that there was no school for the children of the village Tchaikovsky consulted the priest, who told him that there were no funds available. The composer promptly provided the money to establish a school, which was opened in 1886, and he made an annual contribution for the rest of his life. When the school was opened he attended a morning's lessons and said that he thought the teaching methods of the priest and his curate were rather odd!

The quiet life at Klin, however, was no more than a

sequence of interludes in the onward march of the public career. Tchaikovsky could not hide himself away for ever — there were affairs to attend to in the capital cities, and further afield. In the spring of 1886 he went to the Caucasus where he met his brother Hippolyte, who was a sailor and temporarily in port at Taganrog, on the Sea of Azov. In Tiflis, where he met the composer Mikhail Ippolitov-Ivanov (1859–1939), a concert of his music was given in his honour and he was deeply touched by the presentation to him of a silver wreath. After going home, where he worked on the opera *The Enchantress*, he went to St Petersburg, to be met by a delegation of composers headed by Nikolai Rimsky-Korsakov (1844–1908) and to be presented with an award of 500 roubles. This was on account of *Manfred* having been adjudged the finest work of the season.

Meanwhile Tchaikovsky had revised his early opera *Vakula the Smith* and under the title *The Little Shoes* it was performed in its new state at the Bolshoi Theatre, at the end of January 1887. This was conducted by the composer, who was as gratified as he was surprised to discover that his conducting was as much applauded by the critics as his music. He was, said one newspaper, "an experienced and confident conductor, who not only communicated to the players the meaning of his music, but inspired them and also the actors." Not long afterwards Tchaikovsky returned to St Petersburg to conduct a concert of his own works. Once again he was pleasantly surprised that his talent as a conductor was praised. So far to have conquered the terror that used to afflict him on the conductor's rostrum (although inwardly he was very nervous) was a great achievement. At this point Tchaikovsky became a virtuoso conductor, and prepared to take his place on the rostrums of the world.

8. *The Conductor*

THE CAREERS OF GREAT MEN, whatever their function, are moulded by some circumstances over which they have no control. Tchaikovsky was a great musician. He was also a great Russian musician, and in the last years of his life the fact of his nationality was an increasingly important influence on his international reputation. During his lifetime Russia had changed from a backward, largely agricultural, country to a powerful industrial force, with many technological advances achieved, and with enormous potential for the future. In the military field she was also a power to be reckoned with. At the same time government was absolutist, and social progress had not kept pace with industrial. So far from the people of Russia achieving more liberty they could only look forward to the prospect of less under Alexander III. Tchaikovsky, no revolutionary but a man in whom the ideal of a just society burned, occasionally spoke his mind. In 1890 he wrote to Mme von Meck from Rome having heard of the latest stupidities of the censorship: "The spirit of reaction has reached such limits that Tolstoi's works are hounded as if they were revolutionary proclamations."

A patriot, in the sense that he loved Russia and the Russian people, Tchaikovsky suffered much when he contrasted the more liberal attitudes of western Europe with the repressive régime of the Czar, and when he heard, as he often did, disparaging remarks made by western Europeans about Russia.

The place of Russia in European politics became a crucial

factor in the consideration of European statesmen during the last fifteen years of Tchaikovsky's life. At first Russia was aligned with Germany and Austria, and Bismarck made great efforts to maintain a strong German-Russian understanding. This alliance, however, was looked on with disapproval by the French, who, sensing that the interests of Russia and Germany were not as close as might have appeared, helped to weaken the alliance by supporting Russian industrial development by means of trade exchanges and by investment. In 1891 a squadron of the French fleet visited Kronstadt, and the Czar stood to attention as the *Marseillaise* (a song of liberty, and republicanism) was played by naval bands.

The music of Tchaikovsky became a factor in all of this — even if only in a small way. It enjoyed a European reputation on its own merits; but in the last years of his life the composer was honoured sometimes for other than purely musical reasons. By the same token, criticisms of his works were sometimes inspired by feelings originating from other than purely musical sources. French critics tended to accuse Tchaikovsky of being too German; German critics to write him down because of too evident French influences; in Bohemia he was excessively praised as a great exponent of Slavic ideas in music; in Britain and America, on the other hand, Tchaikovsky's works were acclaimed for no other reason than that they were thought to be good music. In these countries the excitements of Tchaikovsky's orchestration, and the deep feeling contained in his music, had the attraction of the exotic. But this was tempered by the fact that this music in some respects was not too far away from the standards of classical music as understood by music-lovers rather than critics.

Bearing in mind what has been said about the relationship between France and Russia it is interesting to note that in 1885 a Paris music publisher, Felix Mackar, bought from the Russian publishing house of Yurgenson the exclusive rights in Tchaikovsky's works in France. For these rights he paid 20,000 francs, of which half, by the generosity of Yurgenson, went to Tchaikovsky. Already an honorary member of several French music societies Tchaikovsky was persuaded to join the Society of Composers and Publishers — an organisation to protect the rights of both parties. Thus he had a considerable stake in France, and the French in him.

News of Tchaikovsky's success as a conductor spread abroad and at the end of 1887 he set off on the first of his international tours. He visited Leipzig where he conducted concerts played by the Gewandhaus Orchestra, which he found much more polished than even the best orchestras in Russia. In Leipzig he made the acquaintance of many musicians anxious to meet him. These included Brahms, Edvard Grieg (1843–1907), from Norway, and Ethel Smyth (1858–1944), from England. Since we are often inclined to idealise "great men" it is interesting and amusing to read Tchaikovsky's pen-picture of Brahms—as "a little man, with a red face, and a huge paunch, who was in the habit of drinking too much." Both Grieg and his wife, on the other hand, he thought charming.

From Leipzig he went to Hamburg for his next important engagements. There he presented the *Serenade for Strings* (op. 48), the First Piano Concerto, and the Theme and Variations from the Third Suite for Orchestra in G major (op. 35). During the last movement of the variations some of the audience ostentatiously left the hall—the music was too noisy! This became the main charge of the Hamburg critics against Tchaikovsky—that his orchestration was unrefined. This so-called lack of refinement is partly due to Tchaikovsky's love of percussion instruments. Certainly he uses them to build up climaxes, but his exploitation of a wide range of effects is to be noted as a prelude to twentieth-century attitudes to percussion scoring. It is worthwhile noting what he can do with such obvious instruments as the triangle and the bass drum.

The chairman of the Hamburg Philharmonic Society begged the composer to leave Russia and to settle in Germany. It was not Tchaikovsky's fault, said the well-meaning chairman with a delightful lack of tact, that he had been born in an "unenlightened country so inferior to Germany"; and residence in Germany, and attention to the high standards of German culture, would correct his faults and turn him into a "good German composer".

That was precisely the point of view against which every non-German composer of any independence at that time rebelled.

In Berlin, however, the audience took a distinct liking to Tchaikovsky's noisier orchestration, and the *1812 Overture* scored an enormous success. After some time in Germany Tchaikovsky went to Prague, where he was greeted with warm enthusiasm by Antonin Dvořák (1841–1904). The way in which he and his music were received by the Czechs, who made no secret of their friendship for the Russian people and their distaste for their Austrian rulers, touched Tchaikovsky greatly. He was fêted, presented to Ambassadors, entertained at splendid banquets, and sent on his way to France garlanded with flowers. He was deeply hurt, however, that the Russian newspapers made no mention of his success.

In Paris Tchaikovsky was the centre of attraction for musicians both professional and amateur, wealthy patrons (one of whom hired a symphony orchestra for Tchaikovsky to conduct at his home), members of newly founded Franco-Russian associations, and those with political interests. The Russian Embassy also gave a reception in his honour. The only sour note was struck by the music critics, who, more nationalist even than the Russian nationalists, generally stated a preference for the works of Borodin, Rimsky-Korsakov, Cui, and Anatoli Liadov (1855–1914) rather than for those of Tchaikovsky.

Many composers found the sea-crossing to England a fearsome experience. Like Haydn and Wagner, Tchaikovsky was glad when he was safely on English soil. He was somewhat put off by the fact that nobody met him and that, when he reached London, no one bothered to greet him. But all the warmth that he had missed on his arrival had been saved up for his concert at St James's Hall. After conducting the *Serenade* and the Theme and Variations from the Third Suite he was called back to the platform time after time. The only complaint was that he had not presented any major work. What a pity it was, said the newspapers, that he had not given London the opportunity to hear the Fourth Symphony. The reason was simple; there was not sufficient time for rehearsal of a work which then appeared so complex and so difficult.

Tchaikovsky next went back to Russia, having heard during his travels that the Czar had bestowed on him a State Pension of 3,000 roubles. He was now independent. This was as well, for in 1890 his patroness of thirteen years, Mme von Meck, for reasons which have never been made clear, withdrew her subsidy. Deeply hurt Tchaikovsky had no more contact with her during his life, although he remained on the friendliest of terms with members of her family, which was, as has been seen, linked to his own by marriage.

In 1889 Tchaikovsky undertook a second European tour, and two years later he went to the United States, at the invitation of Walter Damrosch, the conductor of the New York Symphony Society. The occasion that prompted the invitation was the opening of the new Carnegie Hall. Tchaikovsky, saddened by the death of his sister, was nervous before he started and more so during a stormy voyage in the *Bretagne*. He was overwhelmed by New York; by its size and bustle, its contrasts of poverty and immense wealth, its mixed population, the enthusiasm, energy, and warm hospitality of its citizens. In addition to conducting concerts during the Festival that marked the opening of Carnegie Hall, Tchaikovsky, unwillingly—because he was exhausted—undertook engagements that had been arranged for him in Baltimore and Washington.

The *New York Herald* listed Tchaikovsky with the greatest of then living geniuses—Thomas Edison, Tolstoi, Henrik Ibsen, Herbert Spencer, Sarah Bernhardt, Dvořák, and Bismarck. Tchaikovsky, who had celebrated his fifty-first birthday in the U.S.A., sailed back to Europe in the *Prince Bismarck*. Although by modern standards a relatively young man, he seemed to be old—far older than his years.

In 1892 there were further welcoming noises from New York, but Tchaikovsky was not prepared to face the Atlantic crossing again—not even for the offer of a three months' contract. Nonetheless, he once more made a grand European tour, interrupted by engagements in Russia: Warsaw; Hamburg, where Gustav Mahler (1860–1911) conducted a superb performance of *Eugene Onegin*; Paris; Brussels; London and Cambridge. Mahler became a devoted admirer of the music of Tchaikovsky and conducted many memorable performances of his works. The character of Tchaikovsky's music may be heard to have rubbed off on to that of Mahler, which, in its own way, similarly explores the range and nature of human experience in terms that are understandable by the many rather than the few. At a dinner in London Tchaikovsky sat next to Walter Damrosch, who, hearing that he intended a Sixth Symphony, asked permission to conduct its first performance in New York.

At Cambridge Tchaikovsky received the high honour of an honorary Doctorate in Music, and at a special concert conducted his fantasia *Francesca da Rimini* (op. 32). The

Cambridge function was to mark the Jubilee of the University Musical Society, and a number of European composers received honorary degrees as well as Tchaikovsky. Someone remarked of him that he looked like an ambassador, in contrast to Max Bruch (1838–1920), who resembled "a prosperous store-keeper from the Middle West."

9. *Master of Ballet*

ON May 17, 1892, Tchaikovsky had moved into another house in Klin that had attracted him. This was his last home, and today it is carefully maintained as a national institution by the Soviet government. Although in his last years Tchaikovsky was often abroad, his heart was always in his own country. During these years he composed some of his most famous works. These included the operas *The Queen of Spades* (op. 68) and *Iolanthe* (op. 69). The former, written at great speed and within four months, was to a libretto by Modest Tchaikovsky, based on a story by Pushkin. *Iolanthe* was taken from a popular play by the Danish-Jewish writer, Henrik Hertz, and once again the libretto was the work of Modest, whose literary talents Peter had always done much to encourage. In one Act, *Iolanthe*—the story of a blind girl who wills herself to see—is now seldom performed, but it contains some of Tchaikovsky's most moving expressions of sympathy with those who, like himself, lived in the twilight between reality and unreality. This is felt at once in the shifting harmonies of the introduction (see Ex. 7)—similar to, but simpler than, the chromatic procedures of Wagner. In this way Tchaikovsky suggests the idea of blindness.

Throughout his life Tchaikovsky was obsessed with the idea that the individual was forever fighting a battle against Fate—against unseen, and inexplicable, forces, or circumstances. This is the theme of his operas, and also of his symphonies, and nowhere more powerfully expressed than in the Fifth (op. 64) and Sixth (op. 74) Symphonies. The

Ex. 7

Fifth Symphony was completed in 1888, at about the time that Tchaikovsky was also working on his *Hamlet Overture* (op. 67). When the symphony was played in Hamburg in 1889 Brahms made a special effort to hear it, but said to the composer that he disliked the last movement. So far from being offended, Tchaikovsky remarked that he appreciated Brahms's frankness—and went on to say that he did not greatly care for those of Brahms's works with which he was acquainted. Both men were arguing from wrong premises, supposing that symphonic form was in itself absolute and therefore fixed.

In the end, perhaps, it is Tchaikovsky who has added more to our concept of symphonic music. He was able to do so because he worked on a fundamental artistic idea: that art springs from life. Dimitri Shostakovich (b. 1906) said of Tchaikovsky's Fifth Symphony: "Man, with all his joys and sufferings is the basic concept of this work, which is lyrical from beginning to end."

Shostakovich spoke of the criticism of Tchaikovsky that he was "pessimistic", and suggested that the proper term was "tragic". He went on to say: "Like the Greek tragedians [he] was sensitive to the tragedy, the conflict in the development of human life, both personal and social. . . . His most tragic works are permeated with the spirit of struggle, the striving to overcome the blind elemental forces."

This is the temper of the last, Sixth, Symphony, known as the "Pathetic". Finished shortly before his death, contrived in a grand exposition of tragic emotions after the manner of, say, Schiller, and notable for the bringing together of many non-symphonic elements into a symphonic pattern, this symphony has the quality of a Requiem. And this — remembering that a Requiem Mass is *not* the expression of total pessimism — is how Tchaikovsky thought of it. Or so it would seem from his reply to a request from Konstantin Romanov that he should compose a Requiem. He indicated that this was what he was doing. Only it was not called a Requiem.

Now the essence of Tchaikovsky's music lies in its melodic, rhythmic, and tone-colour characteristics. This, of course, is true of every composer to a greater or lesser extent. What is left out in this brief summary of Tchaikovsky's characteristics is — form. For an apparent neglect of formal perfection — according to conventional reckoning — there is the compensation of heightened intensity of melody and rhythm (both strongly influenced by folk-music), and of tone-colour. The result is a kind of vibrant quality — a kind of reflection of human life as it is. Tchaikovsky's music is moving, in one sense, because, in another, it moves, or it has movement. Tchaikovsky composed many fine dances — especially waltzes — and marches, which are from the same origins as dance. His music, whether intended or not, stands in close proximity to ballet.

Swan Lake was an early essay in ballet. The operas have their ballets. Some of the symphonies have been used as the basis of ballets. The *Children's Pieces* for piano invite ballet; but Tchaikovsky's lasting contribution to ballet lies in *Sleeping Beauty* (op. 66) and *The Nutcracker* (op. 71).

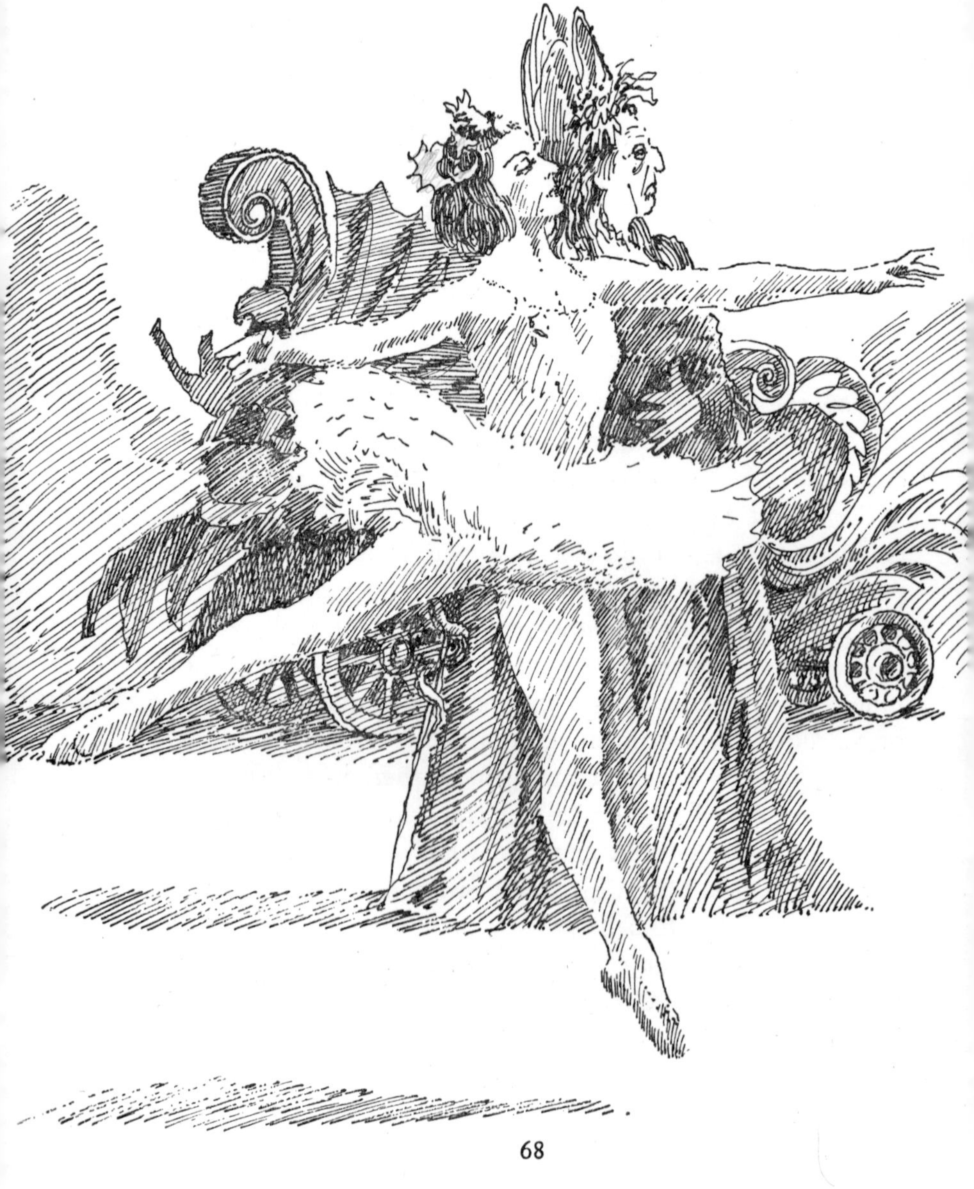

Tchaikovsky, as his intimate friends knew him and as we know him through his letters, was personally a tragic figure. He was, however, a man who loved rather than hated. His greatest affection was for children, and throughout his life he made countless young friends—whose birthdays he never forgot. To them he was a kindly, amusing, sometimes playful, uncle, who had not forgotten what it was to be young. The last two ballets are the works of "Uncle Peter"; and tokens of the hopes that he placed on the future that was represented by his young friends. Although the music of these ballets is not serious (in the way we customarily use the term), it is important. It is the token of a belief in the triumph of the spirit of youth, and in the necessity not to lose faith in innocence. In this way Tchaikovsky links with two important composers of the twentieth century, Gustav Mahler and Benjamin Britten, both of whom look through music at the human situation in a way which Tchaikovsky would have understood.

Sleeping Beauty was the outcome of a suggestion by Ivan Vsevozhsky, Director of the Opera House in Moscow, and a great admirer of Tchaikovsky's music. The story was an age-old tale, and the scenario of Tchaikovsky's ballet was based on the version of Charles Perrault, a seventeenth-century French writer, by Vsevozhsky. The first performance of *Sleeping Beauty* took place in St Petersburg on January 15, 1890, in the presence of Czar Alexander III, and many Court functionaries. No expense was spared in the production—said to have cost 80,000 roubles; and the dancers were the finest in Russia. Yet the performance was received with no more than moderate enthusiasm. The music, it was said, was too much like a symphony, and gave too little opportunity to the dancers.

When Diaghilev decided to produce *Sleeping Beauty* in Paris in 1910 he included some items that had been cut from the St Petersburg production. Since they existed only in piano score, he engaged Igor Stravinsky — a keen admirer of Tchaikovsky — to orchestrate them. In the ballet it is even possible to see how Tchaikovsky himself anticipated the earlier style of Stravinsky, as here, with $\frac{5}{4}$ time, and a brilliant C major blaze punched out by clusters of sometimes strongly dissonant chords.

Ex. 8

"Cinderella" (N°22, Var. 3)

With *Sleeping Beauty*, in which the music of ballet was raised above the level of mere utility and in which the dancers were no longer able merely to exhibit a rather tasteless brilliance, ballet came into its own as a serious art-form. Stravinsky testified to this in his autobiography, where he noted the inspiration found in Tchaikovsky's ballet music by many other composers.

The idea of music based on the story of *The Nutcracker and the Mouse King* had been with Tchaikovsky for ten years before he finished the score in the summer of 1892 after his return from the United States. A suite of pieces from the ballet score was played in Moscow during a series of concerts (containing many works by Tchaikovsky) to mark yet another Industrial Exhibition — this one in connection with developments in the field of electricity. In December the opera *Iolanthe* and the ballet were produced, again in the presence of the Czar. Although the Czar was delighted most knowledgeable critics were of the opinion that *Iolanthe* was an indifferent work, and that *The Nutcracker* was too long. The former work, although much praised in Hamburg after performance there, has long been forgotten. The latter has survived in general on the strength of the short suite that the composer had arranged from it and was already well known when the ballet was first produced.

As in *Sleeping Beauty* the outstanding feature of *The Nutcracker* music is the way in which Tchaikovsky appears able to enter the world of the child — to see things as they are seen by the child and not by the adult. Most of all does this appear in the more fragile and less familiar items of the score — the homely introductory "Decorating the Christmas Tree", with its recollections of Schumann's *Papillons*, and the delicate flutterings of the "Waltz of Snowflakes" (see Ex. 9), which looks towards the figuration of Elgar (whose *Wand of Youth* music has obvious connection with Tchaikovsky), on the one hand, and towards the harmonic flexibility of Debussy on the other.

The most fanciful *Nutcracker* piece is "The Dance of the Sugar-Plum Fairy", notable because of the use of the celesta.

Ex. 9

In 1892 this instrument was unknown in Russia. Tchaikovsky asked his publishers to obtain one from Paris (for 480 roubles) but asked that it should be kept a secret. "I'm afraid," said Tchaikovsky, "that Rimsky-Korsakov or Glazunov will smell it out and take advantage of its unusual effects before me."

At the beginning of 1893 Tchaikovsky set off once again for western Europe. On his return he travelled to Odessa to conduct five performances and to produce *The Queen of Spades*. After being fêted in that city he went back to Klin, by way of Kamenka, to work on his last symphony. This was interrupted by visits to Kharkov, to St Petersburg, and to England, and by the composition of sets of piano pieces (op. 72) and songs (op. 73). Summer passed into autumn. In far-off Chicago an audience went into raptures on hearing *The Nutcracker* Suite. Later in October Tchaikovsky conducted the first performance of the Sixth Symphony in St Petersburg, for which the sub-title "Pathetic" was proposed by Modest. His first suggestion had been "Tragic Symphony", a much better one, but disliked by Peter.

On November 2 Tchaikovsky fell ill. He had contracted cholera. He died early in the morning of November 6. Musical concerts were given in Moscow, St Petersburg, Kharkov, and Kiev. Of these that which made the deepest impression was in St Petersburg on November 18, when Eduard Napravnik conducted the *Pathetic Symphony*. From that day his work took its place among those symphonies which are ranked as among the masterpieces of music not by critics, nor by scholars, nor by musicians but by the judgement of the music-lovers of the world.

This was Tchaikovsky's great achievement; that he could command the attention and affection of the many rather than

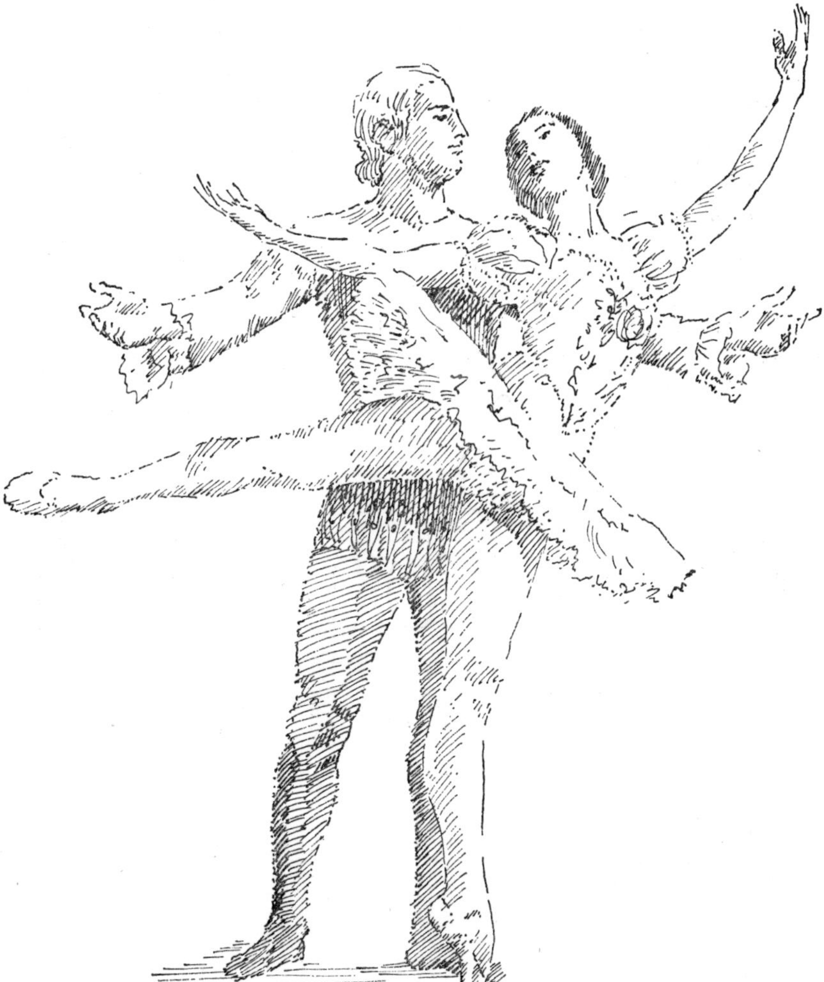

the few. That he did sprung from an awareness of the difficulties of human life—from his own experience but also from that of others, from a devotion to the craft of music, to an intense conviction that music, a universal language, was more than merely a craft, and to an inner faith. He was a humble man, he was a proud man. He was a great man; above all a great citizen of Russia. One song—the "Song of the Volga boatmen"—symbolises to the outer world the spirit of the Russian people through the ages. In this way—in the 49th of his folk-song arrangements of 1868–9—Tchaikovsky gives to this melody a sense of native pride—the pride that he himself felt as a Russian.

Ex.10

Index

References to illustrations are shown in italic type

Alesha (valet), 31
Alexander, Grand Duke, 24
Alexander II, Czar, 26, 48
Alexander III, Czar, 45, 51, 53, 57, 58, 69, *72*
Artôt, Désirée, *27–8*
Auber, Daniel, 19
Auer, Leopold, 50–51
Azov, Sea of, 56

Balakirev, Mily, 24, 26, 34, 37, 53
Baltimore, 63
Beethoven, Ludwig van, 22, 42
Bellini, Vincenzo, 19
Bergmann, Karl, 47
Berlin, 47, 61
Berlioz, Hector, 26–7, 41
Bernhardt, Sarah, 63
Bismarck, Otto Eduard von, 58, 63
Bizet, Georges, 30
Borodin, Alexander, 61
Boston (Mass.), 32
Brahms, Johannes, 60, 66
Brailov, 39, 44, 46
Britten, Benjamin, 69
Brodsky, Adolf, 51
Bruch, Max, 64
Brussels, 63
Bülow, Hans von, 32, 47
Byron, George, Lord, 53

Cambridge, 63–4
Catherine the Great, Czarina, 12
Cherubini, Luigi, 30
Chicago, 73
Clarens, 46
Cui, César, 32, 37, 61

Dagmar, Princess, 24
Damrosch, Leopold, 47
Damrosch, Walter, 62, 63

Dannreuther, Edward, 48
Dante, 34–5
Dargomizhsky, Alexander, 14, 15
Davydov family, 14, 29, 35
Davydov, Alexandra (née Tchaikovsky), *16*, 17, 19, 27, 62
Davydov, Leo, 19
Davydov, Vera, 52
Davydov, Vladimir ("Bobyk"), *45*
Debussy, Claude, 49, *72*
Delibes, Léo, 31
Diaghilev, Sergei, 70
Dickens, Charles, 27, 51
Donizetti, Gaetano, 19
Doré, Gustav, 35
Dostoevski, Feodor, 14
Dvořák, Antonin, 61, 63

Edison, Thomas, 63
Elgar, Edward, 72

Fouqué, Friedrich, 28

Gevaert, François, 21
Glazunov, Alexander, 73
Glinka, Mikhail, 14, 15, 26, 54
Grieg, Edvard, 60

Hamburg, 60–61, 63, 66, 72
Haydn, Josef, 61
Hertz, Henrik, 65
Hoffmann, Ernst Theodor, 28, 53

Ibsen, Henrik, 63

Ippolitov-Ivanov, Mikhail, 56

Kamenka, 27, 34, 39, 52, 73
Kamsko-Votinsk (Viatka), 16
Kharkov, 73

Index

Kiev, 19, 73
Klin, 54–5, 65, 73; *House (now Museum) at Klin*, 55
Kotek, Yosif, 42–4, 50
Kronstadt, 58

Laroche, Hermann, 24, 26, 29, 37

Leipzig, 59–60
Liadov, Anatoli, 61
Liszt, Franz, 33
London, 48, 51, 62, 63
Lortzing, Albert, 28

Mackar, Felix, 59
Mahler, Gustav, 63, 69
Maidanovo, 54–5
Manchester, 51
Meck, Anna Lvovna (née Davydov), 52
Meck, Mme Nadezhda von, 37–44, 48, 49, 51, 57, 62; *Portrait of Mme von Meck*, 38
Meck, Nikolai Karlovich, 52
Meyerbeer, Giacomo, 19
Milyukova, Antonina, 39
Moscow, 11, 22–7, 31, 35, 39, 44, 47, 49, 50, 51, 53, 69, 70, 73; *Saviour Tower in Moscow*, 25
Mozart, Wolfgang Amadeus, 19
Music Examples: from Second Symphony, 30; Fourth Symphony, 41; *Valse-Scherzo*, 44; *Children's Album*, 46; *Eugene Onegin*, 54; *Iolanthe*, 66; *Sleeping Beauty*, 70; *The Nutcracker*, 72; *Song of the Volga boatmen*, 74
Mussorgsky, Modest, 35, 37

Napravnik, Eduard, 73
New York, 47, 51, 62–3
Nutcracker ballet, 71

Ostrovsky, Alexander, 22, 35

Paris, 47, 63, 73
Perrault, Charles, 69
Peter the Great, Czar, 12
Piccioli (singing teacher), 19
Prague, 61
Pushkin, Alexander, 14, 35, 53, 65

Richter, Hans, 51
Riga, 37
Rimsky-Korsakov, Nikolai, 37, 56, 61, 73

Romanov, Konstantin, 67
Rome, 57
Rossini, Gioacchino, 19
Rousseau, Jean Jacques, 48
Rubinstein, Anton, 21, 22, 37, 49; *Portrait of Anton Rubinstein*, 23
Rubinstein, Nicholas, 22–4, 32, 37, 39, 40, 49
Russian country scene, 13
Russian traditional dress, 33

St Petersburg (Leningrad), 11, 12, 16, 17–18, 21, 22, 27, 28, 31, 32, 35, 39, 49, 53, 56, 69, 70, 73; *Winter Palace at St Petersburg*, 18
Schiller, Freidrich von, 22, 47, 67
Schumann, Robert, 41, 45, 53, 72
Shakespeare, William, 34
Shostakovich, Dimitri, 66
Sleeping Beauty, 43, 68
Smyth, Ethel, 60
Spencer, Herbert, 63
Stravinsky, Fyodor, 49
Stravinsky, Igor, 49, 70
Swan Lake, setting for, 1895, 50

Taganrog, 56
Taneiev, Sergei, 42, 49, 51
Tchaika, 15
Tchaikovsky, Alexandra Andreevan (née Assière), 16
Tchaikovsky, Anatoli, 16, 40, 46
Tchaikovsky, Hippolyte, 16, 56
Tchaikovsky, Ilya Petrovich, 15–16, 21, 23
Tchaikovsky, Modest, 16, 31, 65
Tchaikovsky, Nicholas, 16
Tchaikovsky, Peter Ilyich, as a young man, 20; *in later years*, 58
Tiflis, 56
Tolstoi, Count Leo, 37, 46, 57, 63
Turgeniev, 14

Verdi, Giuseppe, 19, 23, 30
Vienna, 47, 51
Vsevozhsky, Ivan, 69

Wagner, Richard, 30–31, 61, 65
Warsaw, 27, 63
Washington, 63
Weber, Carl Maria von, 30
Yurgenson (publisher), 59

Zvanzev, Konstantin Ivanovich, 34

SET IN 12 POINT CASLON OLD FACE AND
PRINTED IN GREAT BRITAIN
BY THE BOWERING PRESS
PLYMOUTH

WHY NOT BE A MISSIONARY?

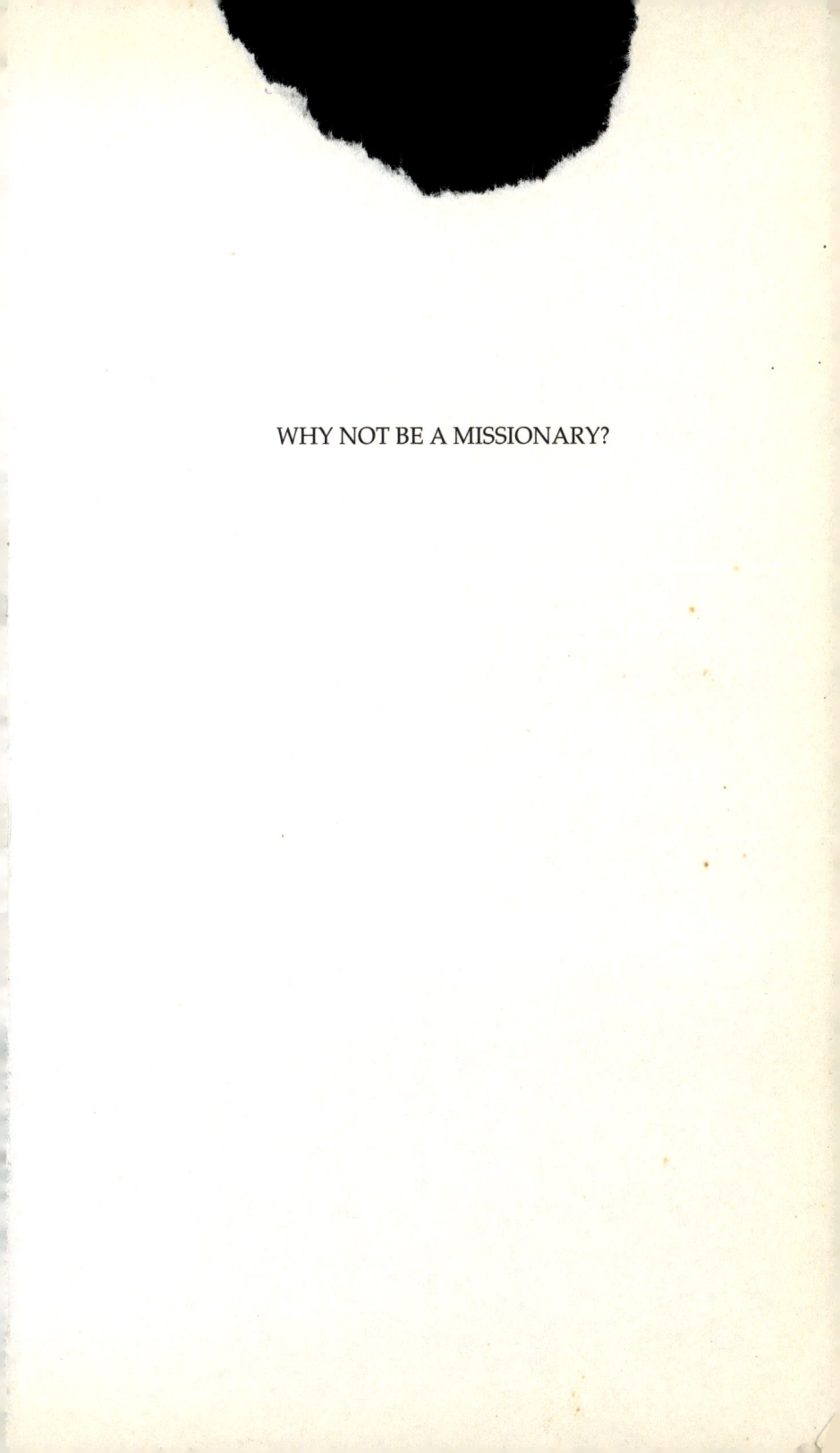